Nashua Public Library

34517011076920

Ancients in Their Own Words
Egyptians

D1456570

DISCARDED

J

Enjoy This Book!

Manage your library account and explore
all we offer by visiting us online at
www.nashualibrary.org.

Please return this on time, so
others can enjoy it, too.

If you are pleased with all that the
library offers, tell others.

@ **Nashua Public Library**
2 Court Street, Nashua, NM 03060
603-589-4600, www.nashualibrary.org

GAYLORD

Ancients in Their Own Words
Egyptians

MICHAEL KERRIGAN

Marshall Cavendish
Benchmark
New York

NASHUA PUBLIC LIBRARY

JUV
932
KER
NPL

Copyright © 2011 Amber Books Ltd
Published by Marshall Cavendish Benchmark
An imprint of Marshall Cavendish Corporation

All rights reserved.

No part of this publication may be reproduced, stored in a retrieval system or transmitted, in any form or by any means, electronic, mechanical, photocopying, recording, or otherwise, without the prior permission of the copyright owner. Request for permission should be addressed to the Publisher, Marshall Cavendish Corporation, 99 White Plains Road, Tarrytown, NY 10591. Tel: (914) 332-8888, fax: (914) 332-1888.

Website: www.marshallcavendish.us

This publication represents the opinions and views of the author based on Michael Kerrigan's personal experience, knowledge, and research. The information in this book serves as a general guide only. The author and publisher have used their best efforts in preparing this book and disclaim liability rising directly and indirectly from the use and application of this book.

Other Marshall Cavendish Offices:

Marshall Cavendish International (Asia) Private Limited, 1 New Industrial Road, Singapore 536196 • Marshall Cavendish International (Thailand) Co Ltd. 253 Asoke, 12th Flr, Sukhumvit 21 Road, Klongtoey Nua, Wattana, Bangkok 10110, Thailand • Marshall Cavendish (Malaysia) Sdn Bhd, Times Subang, Lot 46, Subang Hi-Tech Industrial Park, Batu Tiga, 40000 Shah Alam, Selangor Darul Ehsan, Malaysia

Marshall Cavendish is a trademark of Times Publishing Limited

All websites were available and accurate when this book was sent to press.

Library of Congress Cataloging-in-Publication Data

Kerrigan, Michael, 1959–
Egyptians / by Michael Kerrigan.
p. cm. -- (Ancients in their own words)
Summary: "Offers insight into ancient times through the words of its peoples by featuring modern translations of some of the most important written records from ancient Egypt, including: the Palermo Stone; Stela of Irtysen at Abydos; the Abbott Papyrus; the Stela at Karnak; Tiy's Wedding Scarab; and the Stela of Merneptah, with examples of hieroglyphics and hieratic scripts"--Provided by publisher.
Includes bibliographical references and index.

ISBN 978-1-60870-064-6

1. Egypt--Civilization--To 332 B.C.--Juvenile literature. 2. Inscriptions, Egyptian--Translations into English--Juvenile literature. I. Title.

DT61.K446 2010
932--dc22

2009033475

Editorial and design by
Amber Books Ltd
Bradley's Close
74–77 White Lion Street
London N1 9PF
United Kingdom
www.amberbooks.co.uk

Project Editor: Michael Spilling
Design: Joe Conneally
Picture research: Natascha Spargo

For Marshall Cavendish Corporation:
Editor: Deborah Grahame
Publisher: Michelle Bisson
Art Director: Anahid Hamparian

PICTURE CREDITS
FRONT COVER: Main image, Akhenaten, also known as Amenhotep IV, Pharaoh of the Eighteenth Dynasty of Egypt, courtesy of Peter Horree/Alamy; background image, Egyptian hieroglyphics, courtesy of Gregor Schuster/Corbis
BACK COVER: Stela of Irtysen, 2010–1960 BC, courtesy of Gianni Dagli Orti/Musée du Louvre, Paris/Art Archive

AKG Images: 39 (Erich Lessing), 41; Art Archive: 19 (Gianni Dagli Orti/ Egyptian Museum, Cairo), 21 (Gianni Dagli Orti/Musée du Louvre, Paris), 26 (Kharbine-Tapabor/Boistesselin), 33 (Gianni Dagli Orti/Musée du Louvre, Paris), 48 (Gianni Dagli Orti/Musée du Louvre, Paris), 53 (Gianni Dagli Orti/ Egyptian Museum, Cairo); Bridgeman Art Library: 17 (British Museum, London), 29 (Giraudon/Musée du Louvre, Paris), 45 (British Museum, London) Steve F.E. Cameron: 22; Corbis: 2 (Gregor Schuster), 6/7 (Paul C. Pet), 8 (Werner Forman Archive), 11 (Gianni Dagli Orti), 15 (Werner Forman Archive), 30 (Gianni Dagli Orti), 31 (Werner Forman Archive), 32 (Sandro Vannini), 47 (Gianni Dagli Orti), 55 (Sandro Vannini); De Agostini Picture Library: 3 (G. Sioen), 13, 14 (C. Sappa), 25 (G. Sioen), 34 (A. Dagli Orti), 35 (G. Sioen), 38 (G. Lovera), 54 (G. Dagli Orti), 58 (G. Dagli Orti) Getty Images: 12 (O. Louis Mazzatenta), 20 (Kenneth Garrett/National Geographic), 37 (Bridgeman Art Library), 43t (Bridgeman Art Library) iStockphoto: 28 (Sandra vom Stein), 43b (Clown and the King); David Liam Moran: 18, 23; Photos.com: 57; Photos12.com: 59 (ARJ); Public Domain: 50 Rama: 42; Scala Archives: 49 (Metropolitan Museum of Art); Stock.xchng: 5 & 27 (Alex Bruda); Hedwig Storch: 51; Werner Forman Archive: 9 (Egyptian Museum, Cairo), 10 (Egyptian Museum, Cairo); Zureks: 46

Printed in China
1 3 5 6 4 2

CONTENTS

INTRODUCTION

FIFTEEN THOUSAND YEARS AGO OR MORE, nomadic peoples were hunting, fishing, and gathering plant foods in Egypt. But the earliest evidence of humans developing a settled lifestyle is found not in the Nile Valley but in the Sahara region to the west. At that time this area was open grassland on which cattle could be grazed and not the arid desert that it is now.

Changes in the climate in about 5000 BCE changed everything. The Sahara region rapidly dried out, so people drifted eastward to the lands along the Nile River. There they found a new way of living, not as herdsmen but as farmers. Here they also developed their skills as engineers. Each year, when the snows in the mountains melted, the Nile flooded. The Egyptians learned to capture and direct this precious water by building embankments and channels. The floodwater brought with it rich mud from upstream, which renewed the soils and kept the land fertile.

Kingdom of the Pharaohs

Agriculture was so productive that—most years—a surplus could be produced. This meant people did not have to spend their whole lives ensuring there would be a supply of food in order to survive. Labor could be spared for building projects and creating beautiful craftwork for increasingly powerful lines of kings, called the pharaohs. The pharaohs had huge palaces and pyramids built for them. Soon the whole population had been organized so that everyone had his or her place. Most people worked on the land and paid taxes to the pharaoh in the form of grain.

A Written Record

To keep track of his revenues and to make sure everything was in order, the pharaoh had an army of scribes. They wrote using a script called hieroglyphics. The script was made up of little pictures, sometimes of the things they represented, or they were visual jokes of other words that simply sounded like those things. Mastering this sort of writing took years, and it also took a long time to write anything down, so hieroglyphics were reserved for the most formal inscriptions. A more fluent version was also developed. This was known as hieratic script. Even though it was based on hieroglyphics, an experienced scribe could write it more quickly.

◀ A sphinx gazes across the Egyptian desert, backed by the massive mound of the Great Pyramid at Giza, built in 2560 BCE.

THE NARMER PALETTE

A KING RAISES HIS ARM TO STRIKE HIS CONQUERED CAPTIVE DEAD.
THE BEHEADED BODIES OF EXECUTED PRISONERS OF WAR ARE
LINED UP IN ROWS. SUCH IT SEEMS WAS THE BLOOD-SPATTERED
BIRTH OF ANCIENT EGYPT.

Archaeologists began excavating Hierakonpolis in the 1890s. Their first finds indicated that this had been an important ceremonial center in the days of the Second Dynasty, at the beginning of the third millennium BCE. By 1897, however, they were unearthing evidence that the site had been occupied even earlier.

Modern archaeologists had followed the records of the Egyptians themselves in measuring out Egyptian history in the recorded reigns of individual pharaohs and their dynasties. But these finds dated Egyptian history back still further, into times before the dynasties began.

An Ancient Execution

Perhaps the most striking discovery was a flattened plate that came to be called the Narmer Palette. In modern times we are more familiar with the lightweight wooden palettes used by artists for mixing their paints. Egyptian priests, however, had special ceremonial palettes made of stone, which they used for grinding up powders for making incense or other religious offerings.

◀ This beautiful basalt figure gives us a human face to portray Egypt before the dynasties. Archaeologists believe it was created some time around 3300 BCE.

THE INSCRIPTION

Experts think this is the front of the palette showing a pair of "serpopards," half-leopard (or perhaps lioness) and half-snake.

They face each other, their long, entwined serpents' necks enclosing a rounded area, which may have been where substances were actually ground.

These serpopards may make a puzzling sight for us, but the scene above is more disturbing. People who appear to be prisoners of war are arranged in rows, and they seem to have been beheaded by their captors.

▶ We can guess at some of the meanings, but much of the symbolism is still mysterious to us. The palette dates from the earliest age of the pharaohs of Egypt.

WHAT DOES IT MEAN?

The pictures on the palette symbolize the unification of Upper and Lower Egypt into a single state. This makes Narmer the first pharaoh whose existence we can be sure of.

◄ The back of the palette shows Narmer striking a kneeling prisoner. It makes a brutal image to symbolize the triumph of Upper over Lower Egypt, of civilization over primitive culture, of order over chaos.

with a club raised high, on the point of personally executing a kneeling captive. Beneath his feet are the bodies of others who have already been killed.

Two into One

Horus, the falcon-headed god of the skies looks on, holding a rope (a symbol of captivity) in one claw. He is perched on top of a clump of papyrus—the long, flat reeds that grew in the marshy delta area of the Lower Nile. This part of Egypt was very different from the region farther up the Nile, and until this point it seems to have been a separate state. The capital of Lower Egypt, called Buto, was situated deep in the Nile Delta. Hierakonpolis was the capital of Upper Egypt. By showing Horus standing on the papyrus bush, the Egyptian sculptor was symbolically showing the defeat of Lower Egypt by Upper Egypt.

The tall headdress of the ruler is the crown of the kings of Upper Egypt. On the other side, though, the same king wears the backward-sloping headdress

The one found at Hierakonpolis was a beautiful example, carved with astonishing skill from greenish-colored stone. What experts think is the front of the palette is shown on the previous page; the other side (*above*) meanwhile, shows a king in a tall headdress standing,

DID YOU KNOW?

British archaeologists James E. Quibell and Frederick W. Green discovered the Narmer Palette during the dig season of 1897 to 1898 in the temple of Horus at Hierakonpolis.

▶ With its hippo-ivory handle and its blade of flint, this stunning knife serves as a reminder that, before the time of the dynasties, Egypt still had a stone-age culture.

of the king of Lower Egypt. Future pharaohs would wear complicated headgear that combined these two crowns. This double crown showed that the two Egypts were unified under the rule of one pharaoh.

Narmer's Name

But who was the conquering king who made two kingdoms one? The palette tells us this as well, in the *serekh* seen at the top on both sides. A *serekh* is a sort of riddle for the reader to figure out. The Egyptians liked to represent the names of their kings using pictures to suggest the sounds. So here we have a catfish (*nar*), above a little chisel (*mr*). By putting the sounds together we can tell that the ruler shown was called Narmer.

Is the way the palette shows the event the way it really happened historically? Some archaeologists suspect that the truth was less violent. Upper Egypt became dominant because it was more successful at farming and producing food and was technologically more advanced. This means it probably conquered Lower Egypt through wealth, rather than through war.

THE FIRST PHARAOHS?

THE EGYPTIAN SCRIBES KEPT CAREFUL RECORDS OF THE REIGNS OF THEIR KINGS. HOWEVER, AS THIS EXTRAORDINARY CHRONICLE MAKES CLEAR, FOR THE EARLIEST PERIOD REALITY TAKES SECOND PLACE TO MYTH.

The Palermo Stone is named after the Sicilian city in whose museum it can now be seen. There are smaller pieces in London and Cairo, but Palermo is the largesty. A boulder-sized slab of basalt, it once belonged to a stela, which would (the experts estimate) have stood 6 feet 6 inches (2 meters) tall and 2 feet (60 centimeters) wide.

A Hieroglyphic History

The inscription describes the two defining rhythms of Egyptian life over so many centuries—the succession of pharaohs and dynasties, and the levels of the Nile flood. Too high a flood could carry off livestock, spoil crops, and, at worst, drown entire communities.

▼ Memphis was Egypt's capital through the long centuries of the Old Kingdom from about 3100 to 2000 BCE. Even in its ruined state, it remains impressive.

THE INSCRIPTION

The Palermo Stone gives a great variety of information about every imaginable aspect of Egyptian history, including:

• A naval campaign carried out in the reign of Sneferu (2613–2589 BCE): forty ships set out to an unknown country and came back with a rich haul of lumber.

• Also in Sneferu's reign, the army mounted a large-scale raid into Nubia, in the hills to the south of Egypt. The pharaoh's force came back with seven thousand slaves and two hundred thousand cattle.

• The beginnings of copper smelting in Egypt in about 2700 BCE, during the Second Dynasty.

• Expeditions to extract turquoise from mineral deposits in the Sinai Peninsula.

▶ The Palermo Stone was carved in Memphis, capital of Egypt's Old Kingdom, late in the third millennium BCE. It was taken to Sicily in 1866.

WHAT DOES IT MEAN?

This inscription shows us how important it felt for the Egyptians to have every moment of their lives accounted for. But where they did not have documented facts, they would make do with myth.

DID YOU KNOW?

The main section of the Palermo Stone can be seen in Palermo's Archaeological Museum in Sicily, in Italy. Other fragments are also held in the Egyptian Museum in Cairo, Egypt, and the Petrie Museum in London, England.

Too low a level was also disastrous, bringing drought and famine. The inscription also offers insights into various aspects of Egyptian life, ranging from taxation and numbers of cattle to military campaigns and building projects.

▼ The yearly floods of the Nile have always given Egypt life. The dry desert starts just a short way back from the river's banks.

Mythic Origins

Even with the help of the other fragments we know of, we cannot tell where the stone's original King List would have begun or ended. The latest pharaoh featured in the Palermo piece is Neferirkare Kakai. The third pharaoh from the Fifth Dynasty, he is known to have reigned from 2474 to 2464 BCE. That is no more than a few decades before the inscription is believed to have been carved, which suggests that the text we have comes from somewhere near the end of the original chronicle.

But the real surprise the stone springs on us is how early its chronicle begins. The text we have dates very far back to the starting point of Egyptian

civilization. In fact, it stretches too far to be believable, because it gives us details of thousands of years' worth of what are obviously legendary "god pharaohs" before it gets around to Menes, who seems only to have been semi-mythical. He is regarded as having introduced the idea of ruling a nation under a pharaoh, and scholars believe Menes is actually another name for the shadowy pharaoh-figure known as Narmer, who founded what historians now call the First Dynasty in 3100 BCE.

Before the Beginning

If we are to believe the Palermo Stone's inscription, Egyptian history began many centuries before this official start. For the most part, though, its account feels more like mythology than solid

▲ Neferirkare Kakai had this pyramid built for himself at Abusir. It was completed some time after his death in 2464 BCE.

history. In recent years, archaeologists have been uncovering more and more evidence about Egypt and its rulers in this pre-dynastic period, with the earliest finds dating back to about 13,000 BCE.

Keeping a Record

It should not surprise us to find the Egyptian scribes so confidently chronicling a mythic past. Their whole culture was founded on keeping records. Anything to do with taxes, tribute, numbers of soldiers and cattle, or flood levels was all written down. Knowing what was what enabled the pharaoh to keep control.

A TRUSTY TREASURER

TJETJI TOOK GREAT PRIDE IN HIS SERVICE TO THE PHARAOHS INTEF II AND INTEF III. BUT HIS MEMORIAL GIVES NO HINT OF WHAT TROUBLED REIGNS THESE WERE.

Tjetji has an impressive memorial. His stela stands almost 5 feet (1.5 m) tall and is beautifully inscribed. In the picture that accompanies the text, two small servant-figures stand behind him, in attendance. That is only fitting: Tjetji was a very senior official, the right-hand man to two successive kings.

Tjetji was clearly a loyal treasurer, and pride and humility go together in his personal testament, which is written out across the entire upper section of the stone. It obviously mattered to him immensely that his masters respected him and relied on him so much. His self-esteem was obviously utterly secure.

THE TRANSLATION

WHAT DOES IT MEAN?
Tjetji's testament comes from the heart, but from the heart of a man whose greatest love was the state he served. What he does not say is as important as what he does say.

66 I was a man beloved of his lord and master, given daily praises. For many years I served his majesty Horus Wahankh, King of Upper and Lower Egypts, son of Re, Intef, while this country was under his authority ... I was his personal attendant, his chamberlain. He raised me up; he exalted me in rank; he made me his right-hand man, admitting me to his constant company in the privacy of his palace. He entrusted his wealth and treasures to me, investing my seal with his authority, giving me power over all the tribute brought in from Upper and Lower Egypt alike—all the good things brought to him for fear of his wrath from throughout this country and all those things brought to his majesty by the chiefs of the Red Land for fear of his wrath through the kingdoms of the hill country. I kept track of everything and accounted for it fully, without ever making a significant slip, such were my skill and reliability.

This made me the pharaoh's faithful confidant ... I am a man who loves good and hates evil, a person beloved by all in his master's house, who did everything he did in accordance with his master's will. I did everything alright...

I never overstepped my authority ... Never once did I act in arrogance; nor did I ever take personal advantage of my trusted position. I improved the functioning of every department I was given charge of... When his son succeeded him ... he gave me all the offices I had held under his father, asking me to continue with my work in them under his rule... 99

▲ Tjetji's testament is written across the upper part of his memorial. He is shown standing below it, facing a second text, which are prayers to the gods.

▼ A servant of Intef II brings burial offerings. This pharaoh fought hard to reunite a divided Egypt, but his successors had to carry on his struggle.

DID YOU KNOW?

The Stela of Tjetji is one of the largest and most magnificent stelas held in the British Museum's collection in London today.

If only the same could have been said for the pharaohs he served so faithfully. For Tjetji's time was what modern historians call the First Intermediate Period, a time of conflict and confusion in Egypt. Early in the twenty-second century BCE, the Old Kingdom had collapsed. The Egypt that Narmer had created a thousand years before was broken up, and Upper and Lower Egypt became separate states once more.

Reunited

In 2134 BCE, the Eleventh Dynasty was established under Mentuhotep I, and his grandson, Intef II, succeeded him in 2118 BCE. When he died in 2069 BCE, his son, Intef III, followed him onto the throne, reigning until 2061 BCE.

But the reality was that through this time the Tenth Dynasty was still very much in charge in Lower Egypt. The claims made by Tjetji's masters that they held sway over the chiefs of the Red Lands (the Egyptian Sahara, or Upper Egypt) may have been justified, but the Tenth Dynasty certainly did not rule the Nile (Lower Egypt). Not until the reign of Mentuhotep II (2061–2010 BCE) did Upper Egypt defeat the pharaohs of the Tenth Dynasty and reunite the country. This is why Mentuhotep II is regarded as the first pharaoh of the Middle Kingdom.

▼ In this relief from the burial complex at Deir el-Bahri, Mentuhotep II is shown conquering one of the peoples of the Red Lands.

AN ARTIST ADVERTISES

THE STELA OF IRTYSEN DESCRIBES AN ARTIST'S QUALIFICATIONS
AND ACCOMPLISHMENTS—NOT FOR LIVING CLIENTS, BUT FOR OSIRIS,
THE GOD OF DEATH.

By the early third millennium BCE, Abydos was celebrated as a shrine to Osiris and therefore an important place of pilgrimage. Osiris was the god of death and rebirth. There was no greater deity, and Abydos was believed to be

▼ Abydos was for centuries one of Egypt's most important and sacred cities. The Great Temple of Osiris commemorated the murder and rebirth of the god.

where he himself had died, been buried, and brought back to life.

Osiris, legend had it, was the pharaoh of the gods. His brother Set, the deity of darkness and chaos, murdered Osiris because he wanted to take his throne. But Isis, Osiris's sister and wife (as well as being the Egyptian goddess of motherhood and fertility) cast a spell to bring her husband-brother back to life.

THE TRANSLATION

The Irtysen Stela shows how far thoughts of the afterlife overshadowed the daily existence of the Egyptians. Every day was a preparation for the hereafter.

"I know the secrets of the hieroglyphs, the workings of sacred rituals;

I know all the magic spells and how they work. I am supremely skilled in my art, and knowledgeable in all its mysteries: I can estimate measurements, cut things, and fit them into place.

I know the right posture for a male statue and how the female should look as well... the squirmings of the terrified captive; a squint; a frightened enemy; the way a hippo hunter holds his arm and how a man moves his legs when he is running...

I know the formulas for the different pigments..."

◀ Set up in honor of an artist, the Irtysen Stela is a work of art in its own right. Beneath the inscription we see the memorialized man with his wife and family.

DID YOU KNOW?

The Irtysen Stela is held in the Louvre Museum in Paris, France.

But the spell was brief and only worked long enough to allow the loving couple to conceive a child. Their son Horus grew up to avenge his father. He killed Set, and reigned in heaven as god of the sky.

Hope for the Hereafter

This story, with its promise of life beyond the grave, spoke powerfully to the ancient Egyptians, because Osiris was seen to offer hope of life in the hereafter. People flocked from far and wide to worship at his Great Temple at Abydos, where they would do anything to win his approval. If they could gain the god's favor, they believed, he would make sure they were taken care of when it was time for them to make their own descent into his underworld.

In the hopes of catching the god's eye and securing his support, many people set up richly carved stone stela around his temple, listing all their various virtues and achievements.

▼ Horus, the god of the skies, had a falcon's head. Here he hands the emblems of office to Egypt's pharaoh in a wall painting from the Temple of Osiris in Abydos.

Irtysen seems to have come here some time around 2000 BCE. His testimony provides a fascinating insight into Egyptian artistic values. Any modern painter or sculptor would share Irtysen's understanding of the importance of mastering technical skills in order to create vivid, realistic works of art.

Skills and Status

Irtysen's stela reads something like a job application, because that is what it was. The ancient Egyptians believed that, after death, everyone (except the pharaoh and his family) was required to work for Osiris, just as they had once labored for the pharaoh while they were alive. For most people, that meant hard agricultural labor or work on construction projects. But those with

▲ A noble couple makes their final voyage from the city of Abydos to Osiris's underworld, where they hope to maintain their privileged status.

special talents and training could hope for something better. As an artist, Irtysen was used to being a privileged person, and he may have worried that his special skills might be overlooked if he did not speak up about them.

Below his text we see Irtysen and his wife Hepu receiving funeral offerings from their sons (behind whom we see their daughter and their grandson). The rod and scepter that Irtysen holds are emblems of his authority as a father. Below this, we see a second view of the couple, this time framed as if seen through a window, accepting offerings that are being respectfully presented by another family.

THE CONQUESTS OF KAMOSE

Two stelae at Karnak describe the Pharaoh Kamose's victories over the Hyksos, who were Asiatic invaders. But did his actual conquests live up to these heroic claims?

Kamose ruled Egypt from 1554 to 1549 BCE. At least, he ruled those parts of Egypt that had not fallen into foreign hands. His reign came at the end of what is known as the Second Intermediate Period, a label that gives no hint of what a troubled time this was.

Asiatic Advances

A Semitic people from Lebanon, the Hyksos had established themselves in the Delta in about 1648 BCE. We do not know whether they came by land or sea, or whether they had even invaded at all. Some scholars suggest that they had

THE TRANSLATION

66 The great ruler of Thebes, Kamose the Mighty, guardian of Egypt, says: I headed north because I knew I had the strength to tackle the Hyksos. Amun, giver of good advice, gave me my orders. My brave army went before me like a searing flame ... The east and west gave up their produce as my army lived off the land ... He holed up in Nefrusi with his Hyksos. I stayed in my ship overnight and in the morning I attacked. I reduced his walls to rubble; I slaughtered his people; I made his wife come down to the banks of the river. Like lions with their prey, my men set about their plunder, taking slaves, cattle, produce, sharing out the spoils, happy at heart ... Reaching Yenyet on the way to the south, I crossed to the other shore to meet his forces, my ships in battle-order, my heroes flying like falcons over the waves, my golden flagship leading like a god....

See, I come in triumph! ... Does your courage fail you, wretched Asian?

WHAT DOES IT MEAN?

Though currently limited to Upper Egypt, Kamose asserts his authority across the kingdom as a whole. This was not a true reflection of his power, perhaps, but it was an important declaration of what he intended to do.

weapons technology as yet unavailable to the Egyptians, such as chariots. They also had very powerful composite bows, made by gluing strips of different materials like wood, horn, and animal sinew together. Yet it may well be that the Hyksos simply moved into Egyptian territory without anyone noticing. This might have been because all eyes were focused on the political instability and conflict in the capital, Thebes, and no one noticed what was going on in the territories.

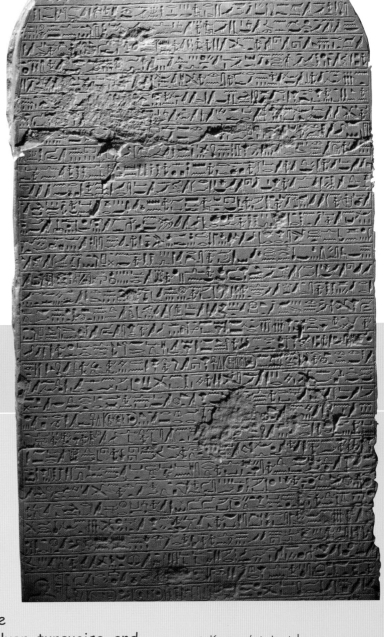

See how I drink the wine from your vineyards, whose grapes your own Asians I forced to tread for me. I demolished your residence; I cut your timber; I drove your women into my ships; I rounded up your horses; I smashed your ships to smithereens and took all the limitless gold, lapis lazuli, silver, turquoise, and bronze axes they had in them ... Avaris ... I destroyed with all its people, laying waste their towns and reducing their houses to smoldering ashes, because they had given their loyalty to the Asians, abandoning Lady Egypt. 99

▲ Kamose's twin stelae set out a stirring account of his military achievements. His claims seem highly overstated, but he did play a vital role in saving Egypt.

25

DID YOU KNOW?

After the death of Kamose in battle in 1549 BCE, first his mother, Ahhotep I, then his brother, Ahmose, took up his struggle. By about 1530 BCE, Ahmose I had succeeded in expelling the Asiatic invaders. Egypt was reunited once more, and the era of the New Kingdom began.

Once they had arrived, the Hyksos quickly made themselves masters of the Nile Delta, extending their territories throughout Lower and much of Middle Egypt. While the Egyptians clung on to power upriver, the Hyksos set up their own state, with a capital at Avaris. They even called their leaders pharaohs, founding their own dynasty, known as the Fifteenth.

Exaggerated Claims

Kamose's account of his campaign against the Hyksos is very exciting to read, but it appears to be enormously exaggerated. He did win victories, but the territorial gains he made were never great. He certainly never reached the Hyksos' stronghold at Avaris.

◀ When Kamose died in 1549 BCE his sarcophagus was placed in a royal tomb, though it seems to have been moved later to protect it from grave robbers.

▶ Kamose had his stelae set up at Karnak, a great temple complex outside Luxor. That way, his heroics were commemorated alongside those of earlier pharaohs.

26

A ROYAL MATCH

THE EGYPTIAN ELITE CONSIDERED AMENHOTEP III'S MARRIAGE TO TIY MISGUIDED, BUT HE USED A GOOD-LUCK WEDDING SCARAB TO SILENCE THEIR DISAPPROVAL.

Amenhotep III was the ninth pharaoh of the Eighteenth Dynasty, and he reigned from 1391 to 1353 BCE. The year in which he was born is now unknown. Egyptian historians were more concerned with recording facts about the reign of a pharaoh, rather than his personal details, such as his date of birth, so this was often not written down. But it is believed that he was still a boy when he succeeded to the throne on the death of his father, Thutmose IV, who had reigned from 1401 to 1391 BCE.

An Unsuitable Spouse?

That makes it less strange to us that he should have married a girl of eleven or twelve years old, which seems to have been Tiy's age when she became his queen. But, for the Egyptian aristocracy, her age was the least of her problems. They said she was unfit to be a pharaoh's wife because she was a commoner.

◀ The royal couple—still together after thirty-three centuries—sit as splendid statues outside the Temple-Tomb of Amenhotep, not far from Thebes.

THE TRANSLATION

66 Amenhotep, ruler of Thebes, given life, and the King's principal wife, Tiy, long may she live. Her father's name is Yuya and her mother's name is Thuyu. She is the wife of a mighty king... **99**

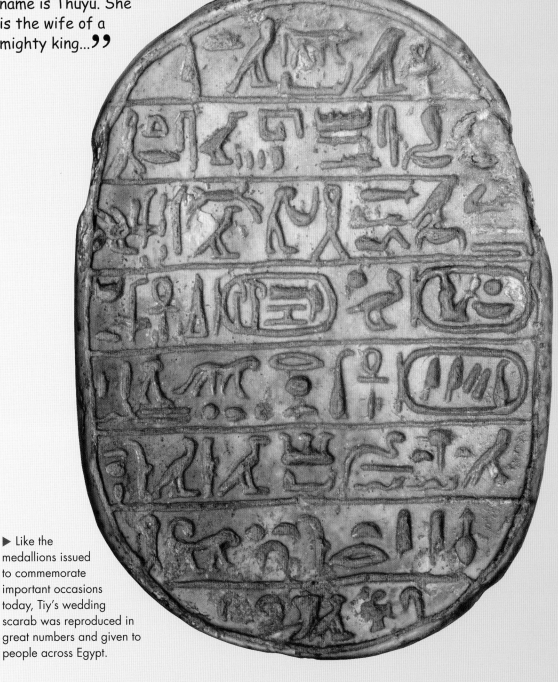

▶ Like the medallions issued to commemorate important occasions today, Tiy's wedding scarab was reproduced in great numbers and given to people across Egypt.

DID YOU KNOW?

Tiy became the first Egyptian queen to have her name placed beside her husband's on the pharaoh's official pronouncements. She was not just his loving wife but his co-ruler.

In truth, Tiy's father was a wealthy man with an important position as a priest. Her mother, Thuyu, was a high priestess of royal blood who could claim descent from Ahmose-Nefertari, the sister and wife of the Pharaoh Ahmose I (who reigned from 1549 to 1525 BCE). After Ahmose's death, Ahmose-Nefertari had even acted as regent to his son, Amenhotep I (pharaoh from 1525 to 1506 BCE) until he was old enough to rule in his own right.

But none of these facts were enough for Egypt's highest nobility to accept Tiy as one of them. When Amenhotep announced his intention of making Tiy his wife, they did not hide their disapproval. But, whether it was because of his romantic enthusiasm or his refusal to be told what to do by anyone else, no one could persuade Amenhotep to give up his plans to marry Tiy.

Charm Offensive

Amenhotep does seem to have sensed that his people might need some persuading if they were to accept his new young wife as their rightful queen, so he came up with what we might call a publicity stunt to win his people over. Amenhotep had a wedding token for good luck created in the shape of a scarab, and everyone throughout his

◀ Tiy was identified with Hathor the cow-goddess, shown here with cow horns. Hathor's milk made her an emblem of motherhood, and she was associated with heaven through the whiteness of the Milky Way.

empire was given one. No pharaoh in the history of Egypt had ever handed out a so-called wedding scarab to all his people.

Why a scarab? It may seem strange to us, but the Egyptians saw the dung beetle as a good omen. As its name suggests, this insect lives on dung. Ingeniously, it rolls it into a ball with its rear legs and then pushes it away to a hiding place for later. Watching the dung beetle pushing along a ball of dung reminded the Egyptians of the way the god Ra pushed the sun across the sky, according to their beliefs. So the scarab shape became very popular for good-luck charms.

A Royal Relationship

In the event, the marriage was a great success. Amenhotep broke with tradition a second time when he had Tiy represented as being the same size as himself in his official friezes and statues. Prior to this, the pharaoh would always have been shown on a much larger scale than his wife, to illustrate his superior status over her. But Amenhotep seems to have seen their marriage as a partnership of equals.

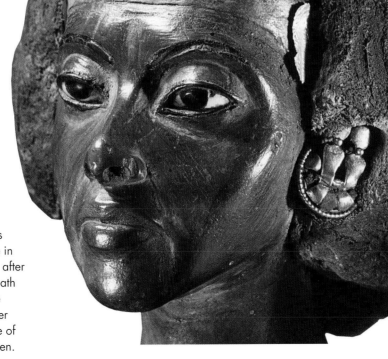

▶ Queen Tiy was a powerful figure in Egypt, especially after her husband's death in 1353 BCE. She became the power behind the throne of her son, Akhenaten.

31

LETTERS FROM AMARNA

LOCAL RULERS IN THE MIDDLE EAST WROTE THESE LETTERS TO SUCCESSIVE PHARAOHS IN THE FOURTEENTH CENTURY BCE. THEY OFFER US A FASCINATING GLIMPSE INTO THE EGYPTIAN WORLD.

Amarna, in Upper Egypt, was once a major city and, for a while, it was even the capital of Egypt. The Pharaoh Amenhotep IV (also known as Akhenaten, the son of Amenhotep III and Tiy) had his home and headquarters there during his reign from 1353 to 1336 BCE.

▼ Amenhotep IV began building a necropolis for himself and his descendants outside Amarna, but the capital was moved after his death and the project left unfinished.

Letters to the Pharaoh

Local people discovered the Amarna Letters in the 1880s. They are not the usual Egyptian finds. In fact, they are not really Egyptian at all, but messages sent to the pharaoh by rulers in the Middle East. This means they are not written the Egyptian way, on sheets made out of papyrus reeds or in hieroglyphics, but in the Mesopotamian way, in cuneiform letters that were cut into soft

THE TRANSLATION

What Does it Mean?

The message the Amarna Letters bring us is the understanding that Egypt did not exist on its own and had dealings with other countries. Foreign policy was crucial in a complex world.

" I prostrate myself at your feet, my lord—seven times and then seven times more. As your loyal servant, I arranged to send my brother with a caravan with tribute to you, but it was attacked and he was almost killed ... Ask your own official if this is not so. My eyes are always directed toward you. Whether we should soar into the heavens or dive deep into the earth, our fate would be in your hands. With this tablet, therefore, I am trying to send another caravan to my lord and king under the leadership of my friend. Let the King be secure in the knowledge that I serve him and am ever at the ready...

Your servant, the dirt beneath your feet, I prostrate myself before you my lord, my god, my sun, seven times and then seven times more. I looked one way; I looked the other: there was no light to be seen. Then I looked at my king, my lord and suddenly there was light. I am resolved to serve my lord and king: the brick may shift beneath its fellow, but I shall not shift beneath the feet of my lord, my king. "

▶ The Amarna Letters were cut into tablets of wet clay. These were then fired (baked) to firmness. Three thousand years later they remain in perfect condition.

DID YOU KNOW?

With nearly 400 in existence, the Armana Letters are scattered far and wide. Examples can be found in the Egyptian Museum in Cairo, the Louvre in Paris, as well as museums in Berlin, Germany, and London, in England.

The writers seem to compete with one another in singing the pharaoh's praises—and in making bitter complaints about each other. King Rib-Hadda of Byblos (a city on the Lebanese coast)

clay tablets, which were then fired (baked to hardness). The language they are written in is Akkadian, a Mesopotamian tongue used for diplomatic dealings across the Middle East. Altogether, 382 letters have been found. Most were addressed to Amenhotep IV, though a few were to his father, Amenhotep III, who reigned from 1391 to 1353 BCE.

▶ Amenhotep IV, or Akhenaten, was one of the greatest rulers of his age. Here we see him making offerings to Ra, god of the sun.

wrote no fewer than sixty letters to Akhenaten pleading for his assistance against the aggression of the neighboring state of Amurru.

Middle Eastern Matters

Rib-Hadda, however, was a notorious troublemaker, and given the number and the desperation of his pleas, it seems that the pharaoh may have deliberately ignored him to make him squirm. On the other hand, Rib-Hadda's rival, the ruler of Amurru, was also pressing in his pleas for support. The entire region appears to have been in a state of turmoil. This is not really surprising. For a century and

▲ Amenhotep IV's city stood on the east bank of the Nile. He intended it as a grand new capital, but it was abandoned soon after his death in 1336 BCE.

a half, the two great rival powers in the region had been Egypt itself and the Mesopotamian city-state of Mitanni. By the 1350s BCE, they had been forced to settle their differences. Both felt threatened by the rise of the Hittite Empire in northern Syria and southern Anatolia (Turkey). But the withdrawal of the Egyptians and the Mitannians from Canaan left a power vacuum there. The result was instability and, therefore, a stream of anguished letters to the pharaoh begging for assistance.

THE ISRAEL STELA

THE STELA OF MERNEPTAH IS NOWADAYS MUCH BETTER KNOWN AS THE ISRAEL STELA BECAUSE IT MAKES THE EARLIEST REFERENCE WE KNOW OF TO THAT NATION.

The Israel Stela stands about 10 feet (3 meters) tall, and was found at Thebes in 1896 during excavations by the English archaeologist Flinders Petrie (1858–1942). The stela was actually dedicated to the Pharaoh Merneptah.

Mighty Merneptah

Merneptah reigned from 1213 to 1203 BCE. He was the fourth pharaoh of the Nineteenth Dynasty, and his name meant "Beloved of Ptah" (Ptah was the Egyptian god of creation). His father Ramses II had

THE TRANSLATION

WHAT DOES IT MEAN?

Modern historians have been most excited about the Merneptah Stela's acknowledgment of Israel, but it is also fascinating for what it tells us about a little-known pharaoh and his reign.

66 He gave courage to his armies in their hundreds of thousands, restored the breath to those who panted in their fear ... he vanquished the Libyans and sent them packing from Egyptian soil: now the fear of Egypt is deep within their hearts. Their vanguard was routed; their legs would serve them only for flight; their bowmen threw down their weapons in fear; running for their lives, their morale failed them and they discarded their water-skins and kitbags to speed their flight.

The Libyan leader, basest of men, ran for his life through the darkness of the night, without his regal headdress—or even the sandals from his feet. Without food or water he fled, fearful of the anger of his own family and of his generals, now turning on one another, their tents reduced to ashes, their supplies seized by our men. No hero's welcome awaited him at home but fear and loathing for a leader marked out as unlucky, damned to defeat by the power of Egypt's pharaoh...

There is rejoicing in Egypt. From all her cities come cries of acclamation for Merneptah's triumphs over the Libyans ... Canaan weeps in her captivity; Ashkelon has been taken and Gezer seized. Yanoam no longer endures; Israel lies devastated, bereft of its seed. 99

◀ The image at the top of the Merneptah Stela shows the pharaoh meeting Amun, god of secret knowledge, along with Amun's wife, Mut, and son, Khonsu.

DID YOU KNOW?

The mention of Israel on the stela has thrilled scholars ever since its discovery. Because it mentions the "seed" of Israel, it seems the writer meant not just the land of Israel, but also the nation. This is the first reference to the Jews that we know of.

ruled for well over half a century, from 1279 to 1214 BCE. During that time his two main wives had borne him many sons. Merneptah had been the eleventh or twelfth of these, so nobody, including Merneptah himself, seriously expected him to succeed to the throne. However, his elder brothers and half-brothers all died before him, so Merneptah became pharaoh at the age of about sixty.

Military Might

Merneptah may have been old, but he was anything but infirm— he was a fearfully effective general. Egypt had been through a period of weakness when he came to the throne, but he restored its military greatness.

◀ Here Merneptah has a meeting with Horus, the falcon-headed god of the skies. This wall painting comes from the pharaoh's tomb in the Valley of the Kings.

This stela was set up to commemorate one particular victory of Merneptah's, which was over the Libyan desert-dwellers and the mysterious Sea Peoples. From the end of the second millennium BCE, these seafaring raiders attacked all around the coasts of the eastern Mediterranean.

But who the Sea Peoples were, where they came from, where they settled, and what finally became of them are among ancient history's great unknowns. They were decisively defeated in 1178 BCE by Ramses III, however.

The Libyans led the attack in this conflict, invading the Nile Delta from the west, near Perire. Merneptah and his men, however, put them to flight. From other sources we learn that the Libyan losses were devastating, and as many as 10,000 warriors may have died.

▼ The Sea Peoples remained a problem. Here Egyptian forces fight off raiders in a relief from the tomb of Ramses III (reigned from 1186 to 1155 BCE).

THE PAPYRUS OF ANI

MANY DIFFERENT COPIES OF THE EGYPTIAN BOOK OF THE DEAD
HAVE BEEN DISCOVERED, BUT ANI'S IS AMONG THE MOST BEAUTIFUL
AND THE MOST DETAILED.

The greatest monuments of the Egyptians are also monuments to the dread of death and to the longing of the pharaohs to live forever. The great pyramids and the painted coffins found within them are evidence of elaborate burial customs. The making of mummies was an industry in itself. Much of what we know about how the Egyptians lived, we have learned from wall paintings and from gifts found in their tombs.

The ancient Egyptians' earthly life was haunted by thoughts and fears of the hereafter. The Egyptians believed it was of crucial importance to get things absolutely right in this life to ensure a better afterlife.

THE TRANSLATION

WHAT DOES IT MEAN?

The Papyrus of Ani shows us how little the Egyptians left to chance where their prospects for the afterlife were concerned. For them, there was nothing more important in life than preparing properly for death.

66 Horus, son of Isis, says: I have come to you, Un-Nefer, bringing with me the Osiris Ani. His heart is good: it has been weighed in the scale and no sin against god or goddess has been found. Thoth has weighed it as decreed by the gods, and it has been found to be true and just. Allow him to be given food and drink and permit him to make his appearance in the presence of Osiris and let him be as one of the followers of Horus for the rest of eternity.

Ani's Speech. And the Osiris Ani says. Here I am in your presence, Lord of the Land of the Dead. My body is without sin. I have not uttered any word I have known to be dishonest, nor committed any deed in a spirit of falsehood. Allow me to be like those lucky ones admitted to your company, so that I may be an Osiris in the presence of the beautiful god, and win the love of the Lord of the Two Lands. I, the pharaoh's scribe, Ani, who loves you and whose word to the god Osiris will ever be true. 99

Mortality Manual

Any Egyptian who could afford it would be sure to have a proper burial. From the many examples archaeologists have found, it seems that they took a special text with them. Today this is known as the Book of the Dead, though in fact a more literal translation of its title would be something like the "Book of Going Out by Day." The book was a guide that told readers how they should handle the whole process of death and judgment.

▲ The hieroglyphic script, in which the Papyrus of Ani was written, combines elegance with fluency. This manuscript is truly a thing of beauty.

▲ Osiris, the god of the afterlife, is one of the oldest know gods in ancient Egypt. Osiris not only judged the dead, but also gave life through nature's cycles.

DID YOU KNOW?

The Papyrus of Ani is sometimes known as the Budge Papyrus because Sir Ernest A. Wallis Budge first translated it into English in 1895.

The Egyptians believed that, after the difficult and hazardous voyage to the underworld by boat, the jackal-headed god Anubis would weigh their soul.

Then, with Osiris Un-Nefer (the god of death) presiding as judge, he would interview them to determine their destiny. The Book of the Dead gave the soul the guidance it needed to negotiate all these steps safely.

Though many versions of the text have been found, the variations between them have been slight. Gaps were often left so the text could be personalized with the dead person's own details.

The Pharaoh's Servant

The Papyrus of Ani is a very fine example. It was found at Thebes in the late nineteenth century and it extends to almost 80 feet (24 m) once it is unrolled. It is written in cursive hieroglyphs—a slightly less formal version of hieroglyphs, which was not as quick to write as hieratic, but for sacred documents like this quite a formal style was required. Using cursive hieroglyphs allowed a huge text like this to be written at least reasonably quickly. Ani, we are told, was a scribe himself. He was one of the

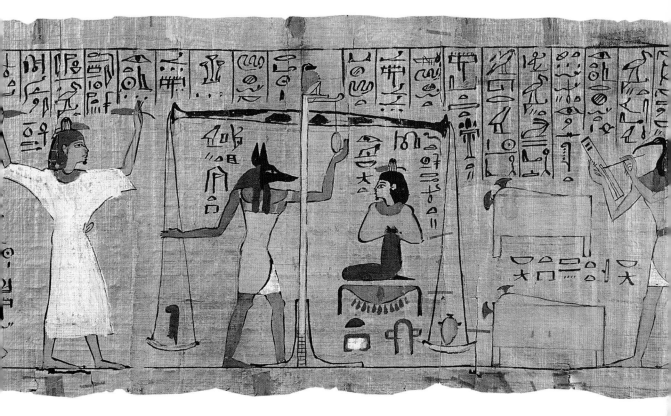

pharaoh's key officials, and his titles were "governor of the granaries of the Lords of Abydos" and "recorder of the taxes of the lords of Thebes." But we are not told which king he served and, overall, the book is very vague about the details of Ani's life. All we know is that he lived some time between 1292 and 1190 BCE.

▲ Anubis weighs the dead soul. Lifted up by virtue, a good one would be light as a feather. A bad soul would be heavy because it was weighed down by sin.

▼ The necropolis at Thebes was truly a city of the dead. Its heyday came in the era of the New Kingdom, which occurred from the sixteenth to the eleventh centuries BCE.

43

THE VIZIER INVESTIGATES...

THE NOTES OF A HIGH OFFICIAL REVEAL A CRIME THAT TOOK PLACE THREE THOUSAND YEARS AGO, WHEN ROBBERS FOUND THEIR WAY INTO A SERIES OF ROYAL TOMBS.

The so-called Abbott Papyrus was originally prepared on behalf of the Royal Vizier (chief official) of Ramses IX, who was pharaoh from 1126 to 1111 BCE. It seems to have been toward the end of his reign in about 1110 BCE that a series of robberies took place in the Royal Necropolis, west of Thebes. Egypt was shaken by what it saw—it was not just a scandalous crime, but also serious sacrilege. The pharaoh's resting place was considered a sacred temple, not just a tomb.

An Ancient Investigation

The Egyptians' beliefs about burial and the afterlife seem strange and remote to us today, but there is something strikingly modern about the vizier's investigation. He plainly understood the principles of police work.

THE TRANSLATION

WHAT DOES IT MEAN?
The Abbott Papyrus reminds us how like us the ancient Egyptians were. But it also reminds us that we should not be too quick to think we know them, because different Egyptians took different views of things.

66 The officials of the great and sacred necropolis were dispatched along with the scribes of Pharaoh's palace and his vizier to check the tombs and burial places of those former pharaohs buried to the west of the city ... The pyramid of King Nubkheperre, Son of Re, was in the middle of being broken into by the robbers, who had so far managed to tunnel two and a half cubits into its fabric ... The tomb of King Sekhemre-Shedtowe, Son of Re, was found to have been broken into. The robbers had dug through the base of its pyramid, from the antechamber to the tomb of Nebamon, the overseer of Thutmose III's granary. The pharaoh's burial place had been emptied of its lord, as had that of his wife, Nubkhas, the robbers having raided these tombs. The vizier, the nobles, and the inspecting officials checked the chamber over and established how the robbery had been effected. The tombs of the women singers from the temple of the Divine Votress of Amun Re, King of the Gods, were also checked. The result: two undisturbed;

With systematic thoroughness, he had his men work their way through the necropolis, checking tombs, collecting evidence, and—at last—making arrests.

Modern Attitudes

Some of the robbers were caught and subjected to torture. Under questioning, it became clear that their attitudes were as remarkable as the police work used to track them down. The tombs were considered by the Egyptians to be highly sacred places, yet the robbers were not afraid to break in and raid them. One robber, a coppersmith by trade, confessed that he had been one of those who broke into the tomb of Isis, the queen of Ramses III (reigned from 1186 to 1155 BCE). "I took a few things for myself," he admitted.

two broken into by robbers. Total four.
As for the tombs and burial places in which have been laid to rest the noblemen and noblewomen and the people of Thebes, the robbers were found to have violated all these, dragging the dead from their sarcophagi and coffins and throwing them onto the ground. They had stolen all the furniture that had been left with them as well as any gold, silver, or jewels, which were in their coverings.**"**

▲ We are used to seeing grand and imposing inscriptions by the Egyptians, but it is intriguing to see the vizier's hurried, hastily assembled notes.

DID YOU KNOW?

The Abbott Papyrus takes its name from an otherwise unknown English scholar, a certain Dr. Abbott. He bought this extraordinary document from a dealer in Cairo in 1857.

▶ A painted priest protects the entrance to the tomb of Ramses IX (reigned from 1126 to 1111 BCE) but such spiritual security had to be backed up by human guards.

This is a very matter-of-fact and calm statement from someone who has been caught raiding the tomb of a queen. The man does sound as though he feels guilty about committing the crime of breaking and entering, and taking property that was not his. Yet there is no hint that he feels he has offended the gods themselves. Does this mean the lower classes did not share the same expectations of the afterlife as the elite? Were their feelings about death more uncomplicated and accepting as a result?

▲ In the confined space of the Valley of the Kings, the royal tombs could be guarded relatively easily. Even so, grave robbers remained a persistent problem.

MAGIC AND MEDICINE

A STUNNING STELA TURNS OUT TO BE AS INTERESTING AS IT IS BEAUTIFUL, COVERED OVER WITH EGYPTIAN SPELLS TO CURE A RANGE OF ILLS.

In 1828 this wonderful work of ancient art was given to Prince von Metternich (1773–1859), a famous Austrian diplomat of the day. It was a gift from the Turkish Pasha (governor) of Egypt in Cairo. No one thought back then that relics of this kind actually belonged to Egypt and so should remain there. Fortunately, Metternich made sure that the sculpture was well looked after, and it is now in New York City's Metropolitan Museum of Art.

◄ Isis gives her blessing to Nectanebo II. The disk of the sun is seen between the horns of the cow she has inherited from Hathor, the early mother-goddess.

Medicinal Magic

The Metternich Stela was carved during the reign of Nectanebo II (364–343 BCE) for a priest called Esatum, who had the stone set up in his temple.

Anyone with an illness would come to consult it, and they or the priest would read off whichever spell looked most relevant to their symptoms. In some cases, the spell would be to drink water that had been poured over the sacred stela.

WHAT DOES IT MEAN?

The stela's spells remind us that the Egyptian medical theory was rooted in religion. Scientific medicine did not appear until modern times.

This is the spell that Isis asks her followers to use to protect against the stings of the seven scorpions: Tefenet, Befenet, Meset, Mestetef, Petet, Matet, and Tetet.

66 Venom of Tefenet, leave the body and return to the earth; penetrate no further. Befenet's poison, hear me, divine Isis, with my magic powers, my words of enchantment. Every poisonous snake obeys me: you must too. Sink into the soil, poison of Meset; rise no more, poison of Mestetef; cease your working, poison of Petet and Tetet. Drop down, biting venomous mouth on the orders of the goddess Isis ... poison give way, withdraw, take flight, and leave the body. 99

◀ The Metternich Stela is part medicine, part magic, and part mythology—a combination that would have appeared quite natural to ancient Egyptians but seems strange to the modern mind.

▶ Prince von Metternich entered history when he brought peace to Europe after the Napoleonic Wars (1803–1815). But he holds his own small place in Egyptology as well.

It appears that the stone's special powers related mainly to the cure of poisonous substances, snakebites, and stings. Around its base is inscribed the story of how Horus nearly died as an infant when a scorpion stung him. Seth, the god of darkness who had murdered the young boy's father, had sent the scorpion. But Isis called on Thoth, the god of wisdom, for his help. He recited a long series of spells over the ailing child. Each charm he uttered ended with a little tag, "and for the earthly suffering as well." This meant he wanted his magic to help living men, women, and children, too.

A Picture of Power

At the top of the stela we see the disk of Ra, the sun, on its nightly journey through the underworld and its rebirth with the dawn each day. Nectanebo II greets it, along with Thoth and some baboons. At the stone's center, young Horus stands triumphantly on two crocodiles. In each hand he holds up scorpions and snakes because they hold no fear for him. He also holds a lion by the tail and an antelope by its horns.

To the right, Ibis-headed Thoth looks on; to the left can be seen Isis. Between them they hold up the walls of what looks like a simple shrine.

Beneath this central scene are thirteen lines of incantations, offering protection against bites, stings, and poisons of every kind. Hieroglyphs cover every available space elsewhere on the stela, describing how the gods dealt with a vast assortment of dangerous creatures.

Not Quite Powerful Enough?

Strong though its magic may have been, the stela was unable to save Egypt, or Nectanebo II. The Persian emperor, Artaxerxes III (425–338 BCE), finally conquered Nectanebo II's kingdom. There were to be no more truly Egyptian pharaohs after that—the Greeks now conquered Egypt, and later, the Romans conquered them.

DID YOU KNOW?

The Metternich Stela is also known as the Magical Stela because of its special healing powers. The ancient Egyptians believed the stela could heal many kinds of illnesses, especially animal bites and stings.

▶ The crocodile is an extremely dangerous natural predator of man, and the Egyptians believed that crocodiles devoured damned souls. Sobek, the crocodile god, was also the agent of Osiris.

THE DECREE OF CANOPUS

IN 239 BCE THE PRIESTS OF PTOLEMY III ISSUED A PROCLAMATION THAT THE KING'S DAUGHTER, WHO HAD DIED, WAS TO BE REVERED AS A GODDESS.

The age of the pharaohs had been brought to a violent end in 343 BCE when invading Persians overthrew Nectanebo II. But just over a decade later in 332 BCE, the Macedonian conqueror Alexander the Great had taken Egypt from the Persians. Alexander went on to add Persia itself to what was by now an enormous empire, but when he died in 323 BCE, it all started to disintegrate. His leading generals fought with one another for the succession and, in the end, the conquered territories were divided into three. Egypt and Palestine fell to General Ptolemy. In 305 BCE he went as far as taking the title of pharaoh, and his descendants continued to rule under that name.

A Protective Deity

The Dynasty of Ptolemy adopted many Egyptian attitudes. One of these was the view that the pharaoh was a god. In the circumstances, it seemed only natural that when Ptolemy III and Queen

THE TRANSLATION

66 Given that a daughter had been born to the Benevolent Gods King Ptolemy and Berenike, Queen of both lands, and since this Princess—also named Berenike—returned suddenly and unexpectedly to heaven ... the Priests ... decreed that she should from that time forward have the glory of a goddess, to be proclaimed in temples the entire length of Egypt... Accordingly, a festival and procession for her have been ordained ... There is also to be a statue of the goddess in gold, adorned with all precious stones in the temples ... there shall be made to her a burnt offering and all the sacrifices appropriate to the days of this feast. 99

WHAT DOES IT MEAN?

Long and wordy as it is, the Decree of Canopus carries its real meaning if you read between the lines. In the way that they write, the Ptolemies are trying to convince the reader that they are not foreign conquerors but true pharaohs.

▲ The Decree of Canopus was trilingual, meaning that it was written in three languages: first in hieroglyphics, then in a more informal Egyptian script, and then finally, at the bottom, in Greek.

The Decree of Canopus is the earliest of a series of three trilingual (written in three languages) inscriptions in the Rosetta Stone series. The others are the Decree of Memphis for Ptolemy IV and the Rosetta Stone, inscribed for Ptolemy V.

▼ Ptolemy III receives the blessing of the vulture-headed Nekhbet, the protective goddess of Upper Egypt. She was revered as "Father of Fathers, Mother of Mothers."

Berenike lost a beloved daughter, they should assume she had been deified and would now be worshiped as a goddess. Young Berenike was now a temple companion to Osiris in the underworld, but she would also be casting her protective influence over the living in the land of Egypt. Issued in 239 BCE in Canopus, a seaport on the coast of Lower Egypt, the so-called Decree of Canopus sets out the ways young Berenike should be honored.

Today we might view a ruler who saw himself, or herself, as a god as being insane or, at the very least, power mad. But Ptolemy III and Berenike appear to have been absolutely sensible, responsible, and caring rulers. And they saw themselves not as Greeks, but as Egyptians.

Famine Relief

The Decree of Canopus is a remarkably long and rambling pronouncement but it makes it clear in many ways how committed to their country the royal couple felt. One section describes the measures they took to help those hit by the famines that had followed a catastrophic failure of the Nile River to flood.

Of course, the inscription is designed to boost the Ptolemaic rulers in their people's eyes, but there is no doubt their assistance helped save many lives.

▶ A European face gazes out at us from an all-Egyptian sarcophagus: the Ptolemaic pharaohs embraced Egyptian culture in all its complexity and richness.

THE ROSETTA STONE

THERE ARE MORE INTERESTING INSCRIPTIONS TO BE FOUND THAN THOSE
ON THE ROSETTA STONE—HUNDREDS, PERHAPS EVEN THOUSANDS, OF
THEM. BUT THE ROSETTA STONE PROVIDED THE KEY THAT UNLOCKED
THE EGYPTIAN PAST.

Napoleon's French forces had conquered Egypt in 1798. The educated officers, at least, were very conscious that they were in the home of an ancient civilization.

However, they were also conscious that the Turks were likely to try very hard to take the country back because Egypt had been part of their Ottoman Empire for centuries. This meant the French were eager to strengthen their defensive positions. In 1799 a group of military engineers were working outside Rosetta (now Rashid) on the eastern side of the Nile Delta rebuilding an old Arab fortress.

Among the rubble in the foundations, the laborers unearthed a sculpted block

THE TRANSLATION

66 Decreed during the reign of the young man who has followed his father onto the throne, the most illustrious king of crowns, protector of Egypt, strict in his observances to the gods, victorious over his foes; the ruler who has brought civilization to all his realms ... Immortal Ptolemy, beloved of Ptah [Egyptian creator-god], issued this edict in the ninth year of his kingship... as King Immortal Ptolemy ... has been generous toward the shrines and those who serve them, directing money and grain toward them from his own revenues, so that the temples—and the whole land of Egypt—might rise in prosperity. 99

WHAT DOES IT MEAN?

The stela itself simply trumpets the generosity of King Ptolemy V for his grants of grain and tax relief to temples. Its significance for us has been as a key to translating other Egyptian texts.

▶ A rather dull text written in three different forms, the same inscription is given in hieroglyphics, demotic, and Greek. The demotic script is recognizably a rough-and-ready version of the much more formal hieroglyphic writing at the top.

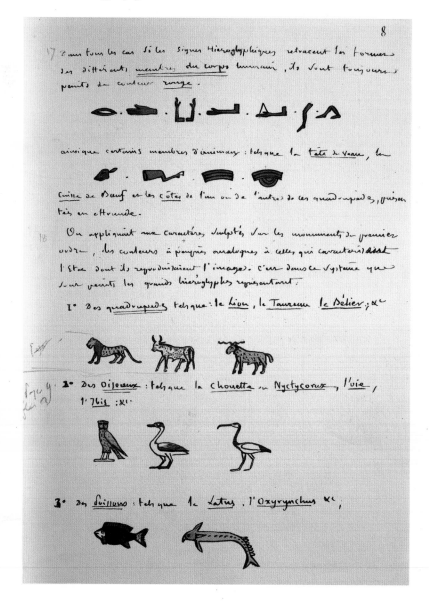

DID YOU KNOW?

The inscription is part of a series of decrees passed by a council of priests that affirm the royal cult of the thirteen-year-old pharoah Ptolemy V on the first anniversary of his coronation.

45 inches (114 cm) by 28 inches (72 cm) by 11 inches (28 cm). One side of the block was highly polished and had inscriptions written all over it. Clearly, this was no ordinary building stone. French archaeologists, hastily summoned to the scene, could see that the inscription had three distinct texts in three different scripts.

What was really exciting was that the third of these scripts was Greek, which just about any scholar of the time could read. This proved to be the key that unlocked the secrets of the hieroglyphic text at the top and of the unknown script that came below.

Tug of War

In 1801 the British attacked Egypt and took it from the French. They saw the Rosetta Stone as a great prize and carried it back to London where scholars set to work to get to the bottom of the mysteries of the Egyptian scripts. But even with the Greek translation

◀ Champollion's notes show how, slowly and painstakingly, through years of patient study, he worked his way toward an understanding of the ancient Egyptian scripts.

to help them, it was surprisingly difficult. With hindsight we can see that they were tackling the task of translation the wrong way around. They were convinced that the hieroglyphic characters were symbols, each one representing some idea. The scholar Thomas Young (1773–1829) actually got halfway to cracking the code, but in the end he failed because this misunderstanding held him back.

Decyphered

The French were still resentful that the British had stolen the stone from them. (It would not have occurred to anyone at this time that the stone actually belonged to the Egyptians.) So it was a very enjoyable moment for the French when, after all the years of British failure, a Frenchman solved the mystery of the stone. Jean-François Champollion (1790–1832) had the crucial insight. He realized that the hieroglyphs were not just pictures, but that the images suggested sounds that went together to make words. After much work, in 1823,

CHAMPOLLION Le Jeune.
Peint par Léon Cogniet en 1831.

▲ Jean-François Champollion was a remarkable linguist who made the crucial breakthrough in translating the Rosetta Stone.

he was able to explain both the hieroglyphic and the demotic texts.

Taking Champollion's findings as a starting point, Egyptologists were able to translate further inscriptions. Gradually, over time, they filled up the gaps in their knowledge until all the writings of the Egyptians were available for them to read.

GLOSSARY

archaeology—The study of past civilizations through the traces they leave behind, including the remains of buildings, pottery, weapons, tombs, and so on.

basalt—Volcanic lava that has cooled to form a hard, dark, shiny stone.

caravan—A line of camels or other beasts of burden carrying goods across the desert in the Middle East or North Africa.

chronicle—A historical record that keeps everything in the order in which it happened. The Egyptian scribes kept systematic chronicles, year by year.

cuneiform—The written script of ancient Mesopotamia, it was produced by making marks in wet clay with a sharpened stick. The characters have a distinctive wedge shape, so are known as "cuneiform" from the Latin word *cuneus*, which means "wedge."

cursive—A simplified script in which the characters can be run together for greater fluency and speed.

deify—To make somebody into a god.

demotic—Literally, "of the people," from the same Greek root as "democracy." But the word is also used to describe a highly simplified cursive script that Egyptian scribes introduced in about the seventh century BCE.

dynasty—A family of rulers, passing power from one generation to the next.

elite—A select minority, considered to be above everyone else in status.

empire—The wider area outside its own borders over which a powerful state may rule. At different times, Egypt ruled over territories to the west (in the Sahara) and the east (Palestine and Syria).

fluency—The ability to use language easily and accurately.

hieratic script—A simplified form of the hieroglyphic script used by Egyptian scribes, where the objects, animals, and people are no longer easily recognizable.

hieroglyphic script—A written form that uses pictures to represent things and ideas. The hieroglyphic script was used mainly for formal inscriptions on the walls of temples and tombs.

Middle Kingdom—A period of stability and strength in Egypt during the reign of the pharaohs that lasted from 2055 to 1650 BCE.

necropolis—A large cemetery or, literally, a city of the dead, it comes from the Greek words *nekro* (dead) and *polis* (city).

New Kingdom—The period lasting from 1550 to 1070 BCE when Egypt had its third and final period of greatness.

nomad—Someone who lives on the move, traveling from place to place.

Old Kingdom—The period from 2686 to 2184 BCE when Egypt had its first period of power and prosperity. Most of the pyramids were built during this time.

omen—A sign hinting at good or bad fortune to come.

pilgrimage—A journey made for religious purposes.

pre-dynastic—Dating from the period before the great dynasties of the pharaohs. In other words, the time before the Old Kingdom. It is a very early period in Egyptian history, which archaeologists are really only just beginning to understand.

prostrate—To be, or to lay oneself, flat out on the ground in a gesture of obedience.

regent—Someone who runs a state on behalf of a ruler who is too young or ill to reign themselves.

relief—In sculpture, a picture carved so that it stands out from its background.

sacrilege—Some behavior or action that offends God or the gods.

sarcophagus—A stone coffin, often inscribed or decorated.

scribe—Someone whose profession it is to write. In ancient civilizations the vast majority of the people were illiterate. The scribes were important, and formed a sort of government department.

scarab—A type of beetle that feeds on animal dung. Also known as the dung beetle.

semitic—Referring to any one of a number of Middle Eastern languages and the peoples who speak them. Nowadays, the word "anti-Semitic" generally means anti-Jewish, but in fact the Canaanites and Phoenicians of Lebanon and Syria, the Akkadians of Mesopotamia, and even the Arabs are of Semitic origin.

shrine—Any place or building that is holy.

stela—A standing stone monument, inscribed with words or pictures (or both).

NASHUA PUBLIC LIBRARY

TIMELINE OF EGYPT

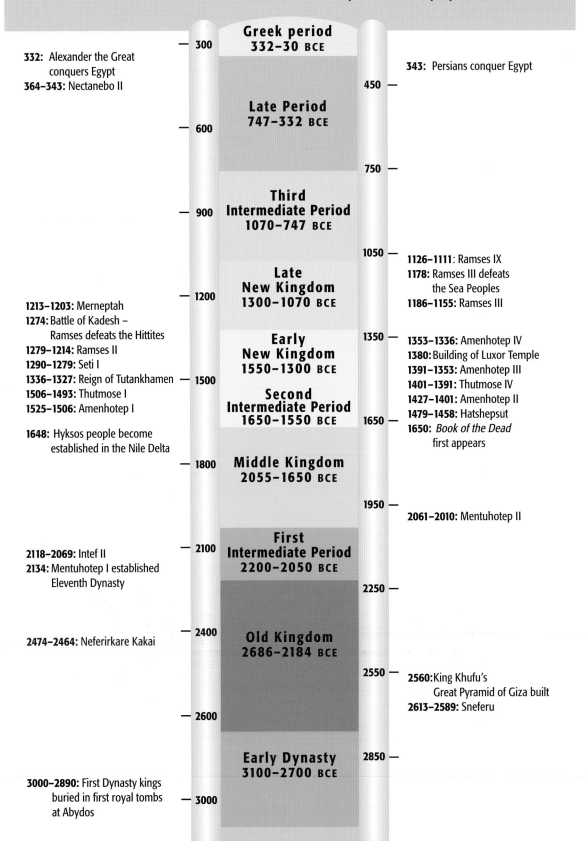

**Greek period
332–30 BCE**

332: Alexander the Great
      conquers Egypt
364–343: Nectanebo II

343: Persians conquer Egypt

— 300

450 —

**Late Period
747–332 BCE**

— 600

750 —

**Third
Intermediate Period
1070–747 BCE**

— 900

1050 —

1126–1111: Ramses IX
1178: Ramses III defeats
       the Sea Peoples
1186–1155: Ramses III

**Late
New Kingdom
1300–1070 BCE**

— 1200

1213–1203: Merneptah
1274: Battle of Kadesh –
      Ramses defeats the Hittites
1279–1214: Ramses II
1290–1279: Seti I
1336–1327: Reign of Tutankhamen
1506–1493: Thutmose I
1525–1506: Amenhotep I

1648: Hyksos people become
      established in the Nile Delta

**Early
New Kingdom
1550–1300 BCE**

1350 —

1353–1336: Amenhotep IV
1380: Building of Luxor Temple
1391–1353: Amenhotep III
1401–1391: Thutmose IV
1427–1401: Amenhotep II
1479–1458: Hatshepsut
1650: *Book of the Dead*
      first appears

**Second
Intermediate Period
1650–1550 BCE**

— 1500

1650 —

**Middle Kingdom
2055–1650 BCE**

— 1800

1950 —

2061–2010: Mentuhotep II

2118–2069: Intef II
2134: Mentuhotep I established
      Eleventh Dynasty

**First
Intermediate Period
2200–2050 BCE**

— 2100

2250 —

**Old Kingdom
2686–2184 BCE**

2474–2464: Neferirkare Kakai

— 2400

2550 —

2560: King Khufu's
      Great Pyramid of Giza built
2613–2589: Sneferu

— 2600

**Early Dynasty
3100–2700 BCE**

2850 —

3000–2890: First Dynasty kings
           buried in first royal tombs
           at Abydos

— 3000

FURTHER INFORMATION

BOOKS

Hart, George. *Ancient Egypt* (DK Eyewitness). New York: DK Children, 2004.

Heinrichs, Ann. *The Nile* (Nature's Wonders). New York: Marshall Cavendish, 2009.

Hinds, Kathryn. *The City; The Countryside; The Pharaoh's Court; Religion* (Life in Ancient Egypt). New York: Marshall Cavendish, 2007.

Rees, Rosemary. *The Ancient Egyptians* (Understanding People in the Past). Chicago: Heinemann, 2007.

Schomp, Virginia. *The Ancient Egyptians* (Myths of the World). New York: Marshall Cavendish, 2008.

WEBSITES

The British Museum: Ancient Egypt—www.ancientegypt.co.uk/menu.html

History for Kids: Ancient Egypt—www.historyforkids.org/learn/egypt

Metropolitan Museum of Art: The Art of Ancient Egypt—www.metmuseum.org/explore/newegypt/htm/a_index.htm

PBS: Egypt's Golden Empire—www.pbs.org/empires.egypt

THE AUTHOR

Michael Kerrigan has written dozens of books for children and young adults over the last twenty years. He is the author of *The Ancients in Their Own Words* (2008), *A Dark History: The Roman Emperors* (2008), and *Ancient Greece and the Mediterranean* (part of the BBC Ancient Civilizations series). He also works as a columnist, book reviewer, and feature writer for publications including the *Scotsman* and the *Times Literary Supplement*. He lives in Edinburgh, Scotland.

INDEX